THIS BOOK BELONGS TO

- -

Contents

Contents

Contents

Contents

Servings	Prep Time	Cook Time

Recipe Name:

Ingredients

Qty	Name	Directions

Notes:

Wine Pairing:

Servings   Prep Time   Cook Time

Recipe Name:

Ingredients

Qty   **Name**   **Directions**

Notes:

Wine Pairing:

Servings   Prep Time   Cook Time

Recipe Name:

Ingredients

Qty	Name	Directions

Notes:

Wine Pairing:

Servings   Prep Time   Cook Time

Recipe Name:

Ingredients

Qty   **Name**   **Directions**

Notes:

Wine Pairing:

Servings	Prep Time	Cook Time

Recipe Name:

Ingredients

Qty	Name	Directions

Notes:

Wine Pairing:

Servings   Prep Time   Cook Time

Recipe Name:

Ingredients

Qty   Name   Directions

Notes:

Wine Pairing:

Servings   .   **Prep Time**   **Cook Time**

Recipe Name:

Ingredients

Qty	Name	Directions

Notes:

Wine Pairing:

Servings   Prep Time   Cook Time

Recipe Name:

Ingredients

Qty   Name   Directions

Notes:

Wine Pairing:

Servings   Prep Time   Cook Time

Recipe Name:

Ingredients

Qty	Name	Directions

Notes:

Wine Pairing:

Servings   Prep Time   Cook Time

Recipe Name:

Ingredients

Qty   Name   Directions

Notes:

Wine Pairing:

Servings   Prep Time   Cook Time

Recipe Name:

Ingredients

Qty	Name	Directions

Notes:

Wine Pairing:

Servings   Prep Time   Cook Time

Recipe Name:

Ingredients

Qty   Name   Directions

Notes:

Wine Pairing:

Servings   Prep Time   Cook Time

Recipe Name:

Ingredients

Qty	Name	Directions

Notes:

Wine Pairing:

RECIPE 14

Servings   Prep Time   Cook Time

Recipe Name:

Ingredients

Qty   Name   Directions

Notes:

Wine Pairing:

Servings   **Prep Time**   **Cook Time**

Recipe Name:

Ingredients

Qty	Name	Directions

Notes:

Wine Pairing:

Servings   Prep Time   Cook Time

Recipe Name:

Ingredients

Qty   Name   Directions

Notes:

Wine Pairing:

Servings   Prep Time   Cook Time

Recipe Name:

Ingredients

Qty	Name	Directions

Notes:

Wine Pairing:

RECIPE 18

Servings   Prep Time   Cook Time

Recipe Name:

Ingredients

Qty   Name   Directions

Notes:

Wine Pairing:

RECIPE 19

Servings

Prep Time

Cook Time

Recipe Name:

Ingredients

Qty	Name	Directions

Notes:

Wine Pairing:

Servings   Prep Time   Cook Time

Recipe Name:

Ingredients

Qty   Name   Directions

Notes:

Wine Pairing:

Servings   Prep Time   Cook Time

Recipe Name:

Ingredients

Qty	Name	Directions

Notes:

Wine Pairing:

Servings   Prep Time   Cook Time

Recipe Name:

Ingredients

Qty   Name   Directions

Notes:

Wine Pairing:

RECIPE 23

Servings	Prep Time	Cook Time

Recipe Name:

Ingredients

Qty	Name	Directions

Notes:

Wine Pairing:

RECIPE 24

Servings   Prep Time   Cook Time

Recipe Name:

Ingredients

Qty   Name   Directions

Notes:

Wine Pairing:

Servings	Prep Time	Cook Time

Recipe Name:

Ingredients

Qty	Name	Directions

Notes:

Wine Pairing:

Servings	Prep Time	Cook Time

Recipe Name:

Ingredients

Qty	Name	Directions

Notes:

Wine Pairing:

RECIPE 27

| Servings | Prep Time | Cook Time |

Recipe Name:

Ingredients

Qty	Name	Directions

Notes:

Wine Pairing:

Servings   Prep Time   Cook Time

Recipe Name:

Ingredients

Qty   Name   Directions

Notes:

Wine Pairing:

Servings	Prep Time	Cook Time

Recipe Name:

Ingredients

Qty	Name	Directions

Notes:

Wine Pairing:

Servings   Prep Time   Cook Time

Recipe Name:

Ingredients

Qty   Name   Directions

Notes:

Wine Pairing:

Servings   Prep Time   Cook Time

Recipe Name:

Ingredients

Qty	Name	Directions

Notes:

Wine Pairing:

Servings   Prep Time   Cook Time

Recipe Name:

Ingredients

Qty   Name   Directions

Notes:

Wine Pairing:

| Servings | Prep Time | Cook Time |

Recipe Name:

Ingredients

Qty	Name	Directions

Notes:

Wine Pairing:

Servings   Prep Time   Cook Time

Recipe Name:

Ingredients

Qty   Name   Directions

Notes:

Wine Pairing:

RECIPE 35

Servings	Prep Time	Cook Time

Recipe Name:

Ingredients

Qty	Name	Directions

Notes:

Wine Pairing:

Servings   Prep Time   Cook Time

Recipe Name:

Ingredients

Qty   Name   Directions

Notes:

Wine Pairing:

Servings   Prep Time   Cook Time

Recipe Name:

Ingredients

Qty	Name	Directions

Notes:

Wine Pairing:

Servings   Prep Time   Cook Time

Recipe Name:

Ingredients

Qty   Name   Directions

Notes:

Wine Pairing:

RECIPE 39

Servings	Prep Time	Cook Time

Recipe Name:

Ingredients

Qty	Name	Directions

Notes:

Wine Pairing:

Servings   Prep Time   Cook Time

Recipe Name:

Ingredients

Qty   Name   Directions

Notes:

Wine Pairing:

RECIPE 41

Servings   Prep Time   Cook Time

Recipe Name:

Ingredients

Qty	Name	Directions

Notes:

Wine Pairing:

Servings   Prep Time   Cook Time

Recipe Name:

Ingredients

Qty   Name   Directions

Notes:

Wine Pairing:

RECIPE 43

| Servings | Prep Time | Cook Time |

Recipe Name:

Ingredients

Qty	Name	Directions

Notes:

Wine Pairing:

Servings   Prep Time   Cook Time

Recipe Name:

Ingredients

Qty   Name   Directions

Notes:

Wine Pairing:

Servings	Prep Time	Cook Time

Recipe Name:

Ingredients

Qty	Name	Directions

Notes:

Wine Pairing:

Servings   Prep Time   Cook Time

Recipe Name:

Ingredients

Qty   Name   Directions

Notes:

Wine Pairing:

Servings   **Prep Time**   **Cook Time**

Recipe Name:

Ingredients

Qty	Name	Directions

Notes:

Wine Pairing:

Servings   Prep Time   Cook Time

Recipe Name:

Ingredients

Qty   Name   Directions

Notes:

Wine Pairing:

| Servings | Prep Time | Cook Time |

Recipe Name:

Ingredients

Qty	Name	Directions

Notes:

Wine Pairing:

Servings   Prep Time   Cook Time

Recipe Name:

Ingredients

Qty   Name   Directions

Notes:

Wine Pairing:

RECIPE 51

Servings	Prep Time	Cook Time

Recipe Name:

Ingredients

Qty	Name	Directions

Notes:

Wine Pairing:

RECIPE 52

Servings   Prep Time   Cook Time

Recipe Name:

Ingredients

Qty   Name   Directions

Notes:

Wine Pairing:

| Servings | Prep Time | Cook Time |

Recipe Name:

Ingredients

Qty	Name	Directions

Notes:

Wine Pairing:

Servings   Prep Time   Cook Time

Recipe Name:

Ingredients

Qty   Name   Directions

Notes:

Wine Pairing:

RECIPE 55

| Servings | Prep Time | Cook Time |

Recipe Name:

Ingredients

Qty	Name	Directions

Notes:

Wine Pairing:

Servings   Prep Time   Cook Time

Recipe Name:

Ingredients

Qty   **Name**   **Directions**

Notes:

Wine Pairing:

| Servings | Prep Time | Cook Time |

Recipe Name:

Ingredients

Qty	Name	Directions

Notes:

Wine Pairing:

Servings   Prep Time   Cook Time

Recipe Name:

Ingredients

Qty   **Name**   **Directions**

Notes:

Wine Pairing:

Servings	Prep Time	Cook Time

Recipe Name:

Ingredients

Qty	Name	Directions

Notes:

Wine Pairing:

Servings   Prep Time   Cook Time

Recipe Name:

Ingredients

Qty   Name   Directions

Notes:

Wine Pairing:

Servings   Prep Time   Cook Time

Recipe Name:

Ingredients

Qty	Name	Directions

Notes:

Wine Pairing:

Servings   Prep Time   Cook Time

Recipe Name:

Ingredients

Qty	Name	Directions

Notes:

Wine Pairing:

Servings   Prep Time   Cook Time

Recipe Name:

Ingredients

Qty	Name	Directions

Notes:

Wine Pairing:

Servings   Prep Time   Cook Time

Recipe Name:

Ingredients

Qty   Name   Directions

Notes:

Wine Pairing:

Servings   Prep Time   Cook Time

Recipe Name:

Ingredients

Qty	Name	Directions

Notes:

Wine Pairing:

Servings   Prep Time   Cook Time

Recipe Name:

Ingredients

Qty	Name	Directions

Notes:

Wine Pairing:

RECIPE 67

Servings **Prep Time** **Cook Time**

Recipe Name:

Ingredients

Qty	Name	Directions

Notes:

Wine Pairing:

Servings   Prep Time   Cook Time

Recipe Name:

Ingredients

Qty   Name   Directions

Notes:

Wine Pairing:

Servings   Prep Time   Cook Time

Recipe Name:

Ingredients

Qty	Name	Directions

Notes:

Wine Pairing:

Servings   Prep Time   Cook Time

Recipe Name:

Ingredients

Qty   Name   Directions

Notes:

Wine Pairing:

Servings	Prep Time	Cook Time

Recipe Name:

Ingredients

Qty	Name	Directions

Notes:

Wine Pairing:

Servings   Prep Time   Cook Time

Recipe Name:

Ingredients

Qty   Name   Directions

Notes:

Wine Pairing:

RECIPE 73

Servings　　　　Prep Time　　　　Cook Time

Recipe Name:

Ingredients

Qty　　Name　　　　　　Directions

Notes:

Wine Pairing:

RECIPE 74

Servings   Prep Time   Cook Time

Recipe Name:

Ingredients

Qty   Name   Directions

Notes:

Wine Pairing:

| Servings | Prep Time | Cook Time |

Recipe Name:

Ingredients

| Qty | Name | Directions |

Notes:

Wine Pairing:

Servings   Prep Time   Cook Time

Recipe Name:

Ingredients

Qty   Name   Directions

Notes:

Wine Pairing:

| Servings | Prep Time | Cook Time |

Recipe Name:

Ingredients

Qty	Name		Directions

Notes:

Wine Pairing:

Servings   Prep Time   Cook Time

Recipe Name:

Ingredients

Qty   Name   Directions

Notes:

Wine Pairing:

Servings	Prep Time	Cook Time

Recipe Name:

Ingredients

Qty	Name	Directions

Notes:

Wine Pairing:

Servings   Prep Time   Cook Time

Recipe Name:

Ingredients

Qty   Name   Directions

Notes:

Wine Pairing:

RECIPE 81

Servings   Prep Time   Cook Time

Recipe Name:

Ingredients

Qty	Name	Directions

Notes:

Wine Pairing:

Servings   Prep Time   Cook Time

Recipe Name:

Ingredients

Qty   Name   Directions

Notes:

Wine Pairing:

Servings   Prep Time   Cook Time

Recipe Name:

Ingredients

Qty   Name   Directions

Notes:

Wine Pairing:

Servings   Prep Time   Cook Time

Recipe Name:

Ingredients

Qty   Name   Directions

Notes:

Wine Pairing:

Servings   Prep Time   Cook Time

Recipe Name:

Ingredients

Qty	Name	Directions

Notes:

Wine Pairing:

Servings   Prep Time   Cook Time

Recipe Name:

Ingredients

Qty   Name   **Directions**

Notes:

Wine Pairing:

Servings   Prep Time   Cook Time

Recipe Name:

Ingredients

Qty	Name	Directions

Notes:

Wine Pairing:

Servings   Prep Time   Cook Time

Recipe Name:

Ingredients

Qty   Name   Directions

Notes:

Wine Pairing:

Servings	Prep Time	Cook Time

Recipe Name:

Ingredients

Qty	Name	Directions

Notes:

Wine Pairing:

Servings   Prep Time   Cook Time

Recipe Name:

Ingredients

Qty   Name   Directions

Notes:

Wine Pairing:

Servings	Prep Time	Cook Time

Recipe Name:

Ingredients

Qty	Name	Directions

Notes:

Wine Pairing:

Servings   Prep Time   Cook Time

Recipe Name:

Ingredients

Qty	Name	Directions

Notes:

Wine Pairing:

Servings	Prep Time	Cook Time

Recipe Name:

Ingredients

Qty	Name	Directions

Notes:

Wine Pairing:

Servings   Prep Time   Cook Time

Recipe Name:

Ingredients
Qty   Name   Directions

Notes:

Wine Pairing:

RECIPE 95

Servings	Prep Time	Cook Time

Recipe Name:

Ingredients

Qty	Name	Directions

Notes:

Wine Pairing:

Servings   Prep Time   Cook Time

Recipe Name:

Ingredients

Qty   Name   Directions

Notes:

Wine Pairing:

| Servings | Prep Time | Cook Time |

Recipe Name:

Ingredients

| Qty | Name | Directions |

Notes:

Wine Pairing:

Servings   Prep Time   Cook Time

Recipe Name:

Ingredients

Qty   Name   Directions

Notes:

Wine Pairing:

| Servings | Prep Time | Cook Time |

Recipe Name:

Ingredients

Qty	Name	Directions

Notes:

Wine Pairing:

Servings   Prep Time   Cook Time

Recipe Name:

Ingredients

Qty   Name   Directions

Notes:

Wine Pairing:

Servings	Prep Time	Cook Time

Recipe Name:

Ingredients

Qty	Name	Directions

Notes:

Wine Pairing:

Servings   Prep Time   Cook Time

Recipe Name:

Ingredients

Qty   Name   Directions

Notes:

Wine Pairing:

RECIPE 103

| Servings | Prep Time | Cook Time |

Recipe Name:

Ingredients

Qty	Name	Directions

Notes:

Wine Pairing:

Servings   Prep Time   Cook Time

Recipe Name:

Ingredients

Qty   Name   **Directions**

Notes:

Wine Pairing:

RECIPE 105

Servings	Prep Time	Cook Time

Recipe Name:

Ingredients

Qty	Name	Directions

Notes:

Wine Pairing:

Servings   Prep Time   Cook Time

Recipe Name:

Ingredients

Qty   Name   Directions

Notes:

Wine Pairing:

RECIPE 107

Servings   **Prep Time**   **Cook Time**

Recipe Name:

Ingredients

Qty	Name	Directions

Notes:

Wine Pairing:

Servings   Prep Time   Cook Time

Recipe Name:

Ingredients

Qty   Name   Directions

Notes:

Wine Pairing:

Servings   Prep Time   Cook Time

Recipe Name:

Ingredients

Qty	Name	Directions

Notes:

Wine Pairing:

Servings   Prep Time   Cook Time

Recipe Name:

Ingredients

Qty   Name   Directions

Notes:

Wine Pairing:

Servings   Prep Time   Cook Time

Recipe Name:

Ingredients

Qty	Name	Directions

Notes:

Wine Pairing:

Servings   Prep Time   Cook Time

Recipe Name:

Ingredients

Qty   Name   **Directions**

Notes:

Wine Pairing:

RECIPE 113

Servings	Prep Time	Cook Time

Recipe Name:

Ingredients

Qty	Name	Directions

Notes:

Wine Pairing:

Servings   Prep Time   Cook Time

Recipe Name:

Ingredients

Qty   Name   **Directions**

Notes:

Wine Pairing:

RECIPE 115

Servings	Prep Time	Cook Time

Recipe Name:

Ingredients

Qty	Name	Directions

Notes:

Wine Pairing:

Servings   Prep Time   Cook Time

Recipe Name:

Ingredients

Qty   Name   **Directions**

Notes:

Wine Pairing:

| Servings | Prep Time | Cook Time |

Recipe Name:

Ingredients

| Qty | Name | Directions |

Notes:

Wine Pairing:

Servings   Prep Time   Cook Time

Recipe Name:

Ingredients

Qty   Name   Directions

Notes:

Wine Pairing:

Servings   Prep Time   Cook Time

Recipe Name:

Ingredients

Qty	Name	Directions

Notes:

Wine Pairing:

Servings   Prep Time   Cook Time

Recipe Name:

Ingredients

Qty   Name   **Directions**

Notes:

Wine Pairing:

Made in the USA
Monee, IL
03 January 2023

24271531R00070